REMARKABLE MIRACLES, UNUSUAL SIGNS

CHE AHN
WITH BESSIE WATSON RHODES

Edited by Frank A. DeCenso Jr.

DESTINY IMAGE PUBLISHERS

authors' own. Please note that Destiny Image's publishing style capitalizes certain pronouns in Scripture that refer to the Father, Son, and Holy Spirit, and may differ from some publishers' styles. Take note that the name satan and related names are not capitalized. We choose not to acknowledge him, even to the point of violating grammatical rules.

DESTINY IMAGE® PUBLISHERS, INC.

P.O. Box 310, Shippensburg, PA 17257-0310

*"Speaking to the Purposes of God for this Generation
and for the Generations to Come."*

This book and all other Destiny Image, Revival Press, Mercy Place, Fresh Bread, Destiny Image Fiction, and Treasure House books are available at Christian bookstores and distributors worldwide.

For a U.S. bookstore nearest you, call 1-800-722-6774.

For more information on international availability, call 717-532-3040.

Reach us on the Internet at <u>www.destinyimage.com</u>.

Tradepaper Edition ISBN: 978-0-7684-1626-8

Digital Edition ISBN: 978-0-7684-1612-1

Originally published in *God's Supernatural Power in You* ISBN 978-0-7684-2832-2.

Remarkable Miracles, Unusual Signs

Che Ahn
with Bessie Watson Rhodes

NOW IS THE TIME

Nothing is more exciting than participating in this move of God that is sweeping the earth. God is releasing signs, wonders, miracles, and healings. The reaper is overtaking the sower (see Amos 9:13) as multitudes are being ushered into the Kingdom. The final preparation of the Bride is at hand—and God is using more than a select few people to do it!

He is using "the saints" in power ministry. As my respected friend, Dr. Bill

Hamon, says in his book by the same title, this is *The Day of the Saints*.[1] Quite simply, we are going where the Church has never been before. It has taken two thousand years to get here. Now we are beginning to understand that *all* of us have the same Holy Spirit and that we are *all* invited to walk in the authority and image of Jesus.

As we look back, we see that God has incrementally restored to His Bride many key truths, such as the knowledge of salvation by grace, the gift of tongues and the infilling of the Holy Spirit, and the truth about and need for the fivefold offices. We have now come to a time in history when the power and glory of God underscore His work and revelation through us. No longer is "power ministry" and the miraculous an occasional testimony; it is becoming a way of life for the believer.

Birthed by receiving God's grace through intimacy with Him, the miraculous is available to anyone who seeks it with a pure heart and faith. We are leaving behind the old "celebrity" model of ministry and walking into the truth that God always intended to have a powerful Church. When He established the fivefold ministry, He commissioned apostles, prophets, evangelists, pastors, and teachers to *"equip the saints for the work of the ministry"* (Eph. 4:11-12). We have spent too many years with *only* the fivefold ministers *doing all* of the work! No wonder ministers quit! A few can't do the job of millions!

A MATCHLESS PRIVILEGE

While there are many definitions of power ministry, my focus is on that which is birthed only through supernatural capability and demonstration. I'm not talking about spiritual gifts, pulpit ministry, teaching, discipling, or prayer. Nor is my focus on outreach or even large crusades, although all of these are of God and require the Holy Spirit to be successful.

I'm focusing now on what I consider to be power ministry: remarkable miracles, unusual signs and wonders, exponential salvation, and visible demonstrations of the power of the Holy Spirit, such as healing.

I also believe that power ministry includes revelational expressions, such as visions, dreams, interpretations of dreams, words of knowledge, and prophecy. Finally, I define power ministry as observable manifestations of the glory and presence of God through the Holy Spirit in supernatural operation. Examples of this include being "slain in the spirit" (falling over under the presence of the anointing) and other supernatural physical manifestations, such as when the apostle Paul was knocked to the ground by God (see Acts 9:4), when Peter walked on water (see Matt. 14:29), and when Jesus walked through a solid wall or door (see John 20:19).

To me, the purpose of each of these manifestations is not to appear impressive to those present, but to glorify Christ by leading individuals into revelation, faith, and transformation. The ultimate goal is the transformation of cities and nations. Power ministry is a demonstration of Heaven's *normal* mode of operation released on earth *now* by those who believe that the Kingdom is *at hand*— which literally means "within our grasp" (see Matt. 10:7).

NOT OF OURSELVES

I know better than anyone that it is not within my power to open blind eyes, to cause cancers to shrink and disappear, to see thousands saved in a day, or to speak a word of knowledge that forever changes a human heart.

And yet God has chosen me as a conduit, and I willingly say "Yes!" What impresses me is not that He chose me or even the degree of power and authority that He allows to pass through my life. Instead, it is the privilege of seeing people delivered of oppression, healed of heart-wrenching illness, saved from hell, restored in relationships, and loosed to live a life that brings Jesus glory.

He has provided the sacrifice of His Son, the grace of the Holy Spirit, and even my desire to step into this place of ministry. None of it is of my own doing.

When I look into the eyes of a person who has received a miracle or been set free, I know that I am seeing what Jesus saw when He talked about the *"joy that was set before Him"* (Heb. 12:2). It is the inexpressible gratitude and awe in that person that gave Jesus the ability to endure the cross. While I have never experienced the degree of pain that He bore,

I forever thank Him for His sacrifice. His death not only gave us salvation, but it also gave each of us the same privilege and grace of walking in supernatural ministry that sets others free.

YOUR CHARACTER

As I asked the Lord what I could best share, I felt it was not as much of what the Lord has done *through* me, but rather what He has done *to* me to allow me to function and be established in power ministry.

It's one thing to start a fire or light an explosive; it's another thing to keep it burning and effective in the long run. I feel the same way about power ministry. It's not just the miracles that interest God—but the man or woman who is representing His name. It is not just the "big bang" of a healing or an unusual sign that impresses Jesus; it is the character of a person that will sustain His glory and bring honor to His name.

Many of us have to learn these lessons the hard way. While we need not falsely minimize who we are in Christ or our authority as believers, our emphasis must always be on Jesus and not on us. The most obvious challenge is to not be impressed with ourselves because He allows us to use *His* power! This even happened to the apostle Paul. He went from considering himself equal with the twelve apostles to finally recognizing himself as the chief of all sinners (see 2

Cor. 11:5; 1 Tim 1:15). Somewhere between these two books of the Bible, he must have had a revelation.

I am sure that, on more than one occasion, God has had a good laugh at those of us who misunderstand our use of someone else's tools when we present ourselves as the manufacturer. I have found that the more God uses me in power, the more humble I become. I am simply discovering that *"...it is no longer I who live, but Christ who lives in me..."* (Gal. 2:20). It's Jesus alone who's "doing the stuff" and allowing me to partner with Him.

WHAT INTERESTS GOD

As revival approaches, many more believers will begin to flow in power ministry. The prophets in the land have been declaring for several years that we are in a time of acceleration. Not only are more people getting saved in a shorter amount of time, but personal growth in individuals and in the Church is also accelerating. In this season, knowing and heeding the foundational truths of character and ministry are more important than ever.

How do you build your life wisely in order to facilitate power ministry? The cost for one who wants to move in signs, wonders, and power is higher than for those who choose to simply be saved and sit in the background. A person "hiding out" until He comes is really no threat to satan and the forces of hell. But those who step into power ministry may easily become "front line" victors or (sadly) casualties, depending on the foundation they lay.

For which of you, intending to build a tower, does not sit down first and count the cost, whether he has enough to finish it—lest, after he has laid the foundation, and is not able to finish, all who see it be-

gin to mock him, saying "This man began to build and was not able to finish" (Luke 14:28-30).

God loves risk-takers and overcomers, and He is pleased only by those who walk in faith (see Heb. 11:6). In fact, the Bible says that He takes no pleasure in those who *"shrink back"* (Heb. 10:38 NASB).

But He also has laid out strategies for us to keep us running the race in such a way so as to win (see 1 Cor. 9:24). You need to count the cost daily and follow His plan in order to finish well.

BEGIN WITH THE BASICS

Early in my walk, the Lord impressed on me the importance of the basics, of prayer and obedience. Both are extremely vital, yet easy to forget.

As John Wesley said, "God does nothing on earth save in answer to believing prayer."[2] Jesus called His Church a house of prayer (see Matt. 21:13). He was consistently praying, seeking the Father's will, rising early to spend time with His Father, and telling His disciples that He did nothing of His own accord, but only what He saw the Father doing (see John 5:19). To only do what you see the Father doing requires that you spend enough time *with God* to know what He is about! Too often, we rush off to do our own thing and simply ask God to bless it on the way. That is not how God intended us to operate.

Nothing has changed since Jesus followed His Father's lead—so it should be the same for you and me today. Prayer gives us the Father's heart and priorities, and it also changes ours. In fact, perhaps the most important part of prayer is that it changes *our* minds, not God's. We become like Him as we connect with Him (see 1 John 3:2). In that manner, we display His intentions and not our own.

Prayer should *be* our lifestyle. Paul encourages us to pray without ceasing (see 1 Thess. 5:17). An effective way to do this is to pray in tongues. Praying in tongues builds you up and assures pure communication with the Father. It gives you strength for the task at hand and often redirects you when you would have chosen to do something differently. We may plan our way, but the *"Lord directs our steps"* (Prov. 16:9).

We all too often decide what "makes sense" to us and rush off to do it without consulting the Lord. We are never so mature that we do not need to pray about what to do and how to do it.

Even King David, wise in matters of war, constantly asked before each battle, *"Shall I go up"* (1 Sam. 23:2). Even when he had won a mighty campaign just a few days earlier, he did not put confidence in what worked yesterday in order to determine what was right for today.

God made manna to spoil if it was used more than one day (see Exod. 16:20). The same applies to yesterday's "portion" from the Lord. We need to seek our new portion each day and let the Lord direct our steps. We often need to stop in the middle of an activity (even public ministry) and pray to see if the Spirit has shifted or is redirecting us to a different method, a time of silence, a time of prophecy, etc., so as to stay attuned sharply to His will.

Continually seeking His face in prayer is not a work of the flesh or something to put on a "to do list." The grace to pray is a gift in itself and part of an intimate relationship with God. I believe it comes by being continually filled with the spirit, as proscribed in Ephesians 5:18. We need to be filled anew every day in order to operate in the supernatural. It is this same filling that keeps us from walking in the flesh. As we daily walk in the Spirit, we grow in the sanctification and holiness that reflect God's character in our lives (see Gal. 5:22-23).

Yet prayer can be virtually ineffective if we are not *obedient* to what God is showing us through it. It may be obedience to how long we spend in His presence or how we care for our family or others in our ministry. It may be obedience in taking care of ourselves or in financial discipline. It may be the small obedience of hearing His voice and responding quickly to His prompting, even if it seems odd or unnecessary. While it may not seem relevant to moving into the realm of power ministry, we must be willing to be obedient in the small or unpleasant areas of our lives. Otherwise, what confidence can God have in us that we will follow Him in bigger and often more crucial instruction? (See Luke 16:10.)

I have found that, in my personal journey toward seeing blind eyes healed, if God asked me to pray for someone with a headache or a hangnail, my refusal to do so would hinder the fulfillment of greater works in the future.

Likewise, if I am out running around looking for someone to pray for at the mall when the Lord has asked me to be home spending time with my family, I have also missed the mark. Though an activity may look good, if it is self-initiated, it is still disobedience.

If God asks you to pick up a piece of trash, take home a person who needs a ride, or give $10 to a stranger, you must obey with the knowledge that these actions are just as "spiritual" as the "big" prayers. God's prompting alone determines the importance of your actions. And He is not impressed when you choose which of His commands you will obey based upon their importance in your eyes.

I have a friend who the Lord once prompted, at a stoplight, to follow the car in front of her and to pray for the driver. She thought it odd and came up with a myriad of excuses for why, as a single woman late at night, this would not be sensible. She actually refused to do it, passing the car as it turned into a mini-mart. As she drove past, the Lord told her, in the voice she had heard so many times before, "If you would just be obedient, something very important will happen." She turned around and went back to the market.

The time was 11:45 P.M. The driver turned out to be an older woman desperately seeking an answer from God. She cried as my friend delivered the word. The woman then told my friend that she was planning to take her own life after midnight if she received no reply from

God. We never know in advance why our obedience is so critical, but God does. We are wise to obey.

FAITHFUL WITH LITTLE

When counting the cost of walking in power ministry, where do you place the importance of keeping your check book accurate, paying the rent on time, giving back what isn't yours, and tithing? Do you think these little duties might be irrelevant when it comes to seeing the lame walk?

It is not so in God's eyes. Luke 16:10 tells us that, if you are faithful with little, you will also be faithful with much. Moreover, Jesus states, *"Therefore, if you have not been faithful in the unrighteous mammon, who will commit to your trust the true riches"* (Luke 16:11). Surely the true riches are spiritual gifts and the intimate knowledge of God. These are priceless to the believer. Yet they are reserved for the one who has been found faithful in little. God is interested in the one who has paid what he owes and considers honesty and integrity in small things just as important as in big things.

The very next verse says, *"If you have not been faithful in what is another man's, who will give you what is your own"* (Luke 16:12). I believe this applies to how reliable you are with things that belong to others—especially in ministries that you may be serving. Perhaps it is another's offering that you are counting, their building that you are cleaning, or a small group that you are stewarding. Do you treat it as your own and take great care?

How you serve others will likely be how others will serve you. Your faithfulness and trustworthiness in daily activities helps determine how well you will handle the choicest of spiritual riches.

You may have heard that what you do in secret shows who you really are. Nothing about us is hidden from our Father, so we would be wise to give a righteous accounting in all that we do. We can find no shortcuts to character. If an area in your life needs special attention, humble yourself and seek healing or restoration so that it will not cause your failure in the future.

Although you may think that God is taking too long to release you to your heart's desire, you must know that He is investing carefully in your life in order to undergird the coming power so that it won't destroy you or others in the process.

If you had a son who showed little responsibility in most areas of his life, would it be wise for you to buy him a turbocharged vehicle at 16 that could cost him his life? Or would it make more sense to help him buy a reliable car until he proves himself able to handle greater responsibility? The Lord, as a Father, has the same prudent affection for us. He cares deeply about our character.

Thus, instead of focusing on the big ministry that we don't yet have, we must focus on the foundation of all ministry—our character. We need to follow through on integrity in large and small things, including resolving conflicts, making phone calls that we'd rather avoid, reading the Word when we don't feel like it, and choosing to honor our relationships and spend time with our families or spouses when we had something else in mind.

A LEVEL AND BALANCED LIFE

Sadly, if we read about many of the spiritual greats who moved in historic power ministry—such as William Branham, or many others who fell—we discover the tragedies that they encountered in their personal lives in the form of alcohol or prescription addiction, failed relationships, the love of money, sexual immorality, false doctrine, and more. Most of their failures were rooted in the pressure to carry the anointing without having true accountability or receiving assistance from others.

We are blessed to find ourselves in a time when the fivefold ministry is being re-established and most church movements are implementing godly structures and apostolic alignment to oversee their ministers and to offer help when needed. This is to our benefit. I would never think of moving alone in the dimension of power ministry that the Lord has bestowed upon me without the blessing of other godly leaders. I want godly men and women speaking into my life and giving guidance as needed. I believe that mutual submission to peers and those more mature in the Lord is an absolute necessity and that team ministry and the counsel of others is wise.

I pray you will make these tenants vital priorities as well. Even as He sent out the early apostles two by two, God is revealing that team ministry is a safeguard in many ways. First, it is a very practical means to prevent burn-out and exhaustion. It is also a great deterrent from satan's traps of temptation and from the assaults of the enemy. Two have exponential power when it comes to spiritual opposition—one puts a thousand to flight; two put ten thousand to flight (see Deut. 32:30).

In the "thrill of the moment," while moving in power ministry, watching blind eyes become clear, a person cast off a leg brace, or a thousand rush forward for salvation, we often forget that we are running a marathon, not a sprint. We are in this for the long haul, while we have breath or until Jesus comes.

That is why balance is such an important facet of our lives. I personally care about you as I write this because I know firsthand the problems that ensue when our priorities are out of alignment with God's best.

These include personal priorities, such as taking care of your body (exercise, proper rest, and nutrition) and guarding your family life. Many ministers wrongly sacrifice their families or their children "for the sake of the Gospel" when this brings shame to the name of our Savior.

My family intentionally sets aside time to nurture our relationships in the midst of busy schedules. For example, after 29 years of marriage, I still "date" my wife on a weekly basis. We also have a family dinner on a weekly basis, even though two of my children are married. Thank God that they live close by and are active at Harvest Rock Church, where I pastor.

At all times, we are *living epistles to be read of all men* (2 Cor. 3:2). Are you living in such a way that anyone would want to convert to what you represent?

The other type of balance is ministry balance. If we are just doing series of "glory" or "miracle" meetings, we must ask ourselves when the infrastructure is being built into the lives of those participating. We are to make disciples, not spectators or receivers. We must teach others the foundations of the faith and the importance of giving away what they receive. *Freely you received, freely give* (Matt. 10:7-8).

We need to be connected with and lead others to resources and training centers and churches as we move in power ministry so that "lasting fruit" can be grown in those who are touched, healed, or saved.

Another important balance is reproduction. The objective is not a few "sainted ones" who are capable of walking in power ministry. Rather, our goal is for all of God's people to walk in the revelation that they *are* sons and daughters of God (see 1 John 3:1). It means embracing the truth that we are made in *His* image and are given *all* of His inheritance. As Jesus said to His Father, *"For I have given them the words which you have given Me…"* (John 17:8). He went on to pray, *"The glory which You gave Me I have given them…"* (John 17:22). We need to *believe* and *act* on the mandate, *"Greater works than these* [**you**] *will do"* (John 14:12). What an awesome promise!

God is waiting for a Bride with whom He can be *equally* yoked, and that necessitates that we walk in some pretty impressive power!

Discerning Good and Evil

It is amazing to me how many aspiring ministers are not well-versed in the Word.

Certainly, this is a cause for Bible Schools, but I believe that knowing God's Word is a non-negotiable for every believer. We must set our focus on the Word to study and apply it all the days of our lives. The Word alone is our ultimate umpire on the truth of what is set before us. We will need that standard often.

Moving on to the "meat" of the Word is especially important. *"Solid food belongs to those who are of full age, that is, those who by reason of use have their senses exercised to discern both good and evil"* (Heb. 5:14).

The Word trains us to walk in power ministry in many ways. First, the Word is a record of testimony. Such testimony builds our faith that we too can operate in this dimension. We can see how miracles happened, when they happened, and who God chose.

Second, in the Word we can see the growth of a minister's life. David did not take on Goliath as his first conquest, but he had already overcome the lion and the bear (see 1 Sam. 17:34-36). In the same way, many are not prepared to pray for a cancerous tumor during their first ministry trip; we start with what is set before us and learn to grow and discern.

Growth in discernment is one of the most important aspects of ministry. God has given us senses. When consecrated and not given over to ruling our spirit, our senses serve as keen guidance in following the Lord's lead.

This is especially true in the revelational and prophetic gifts, such as word of knowledge, prophecy, and word of wisdom. When we have our senses trained, we grow in discerning what the Lord is saying. He may speak to you by pulling on your heart out of compassion for a certain individual (He did this with Jesus in Mark 1:40ff). Or He may speak to your spirit. You may find that certain verses jump out of the Word, giving guidance or insight to your immediate situation. You may receive pictures or visions in your mind while awake or dreams while asleep. Most people experience "butterflies," or an inner knowing, when they are receiving a truth or information that God wants them to release.

As you release these words (and in the process, discover if they are of the Lord), your confidence will grow, and your level of accuracy and reception will increase. Don't be afraid to fail as you share what you receive. Just offer your insights in humility because you are learning and growing in these gifts. No one is right all of the time. The Word says, *"We know in part, we prophesy in part"* (1 Cor. 13:9). We do grow!

The Word provides us with wonderfully powerful gifts. When we read the Bible as our record of testimony, we learn that Jesus' one word of knowledge to the woman at the well brought an entire town to salvation (see John 4:1-42). That is power ministry!

Elisha and his servant's vision of the unseen forces of God gave his servant faith that they would win the battle when they were greatly outnumbered (see 2 Kings 6:8-23). It was pretty important that Ananias received a word of knowledge regarding where to find Saul (Paul) to pray for his sight to be restored, thereby winning one of the greatest leaders of all Christendom (see Acts 9:10-19). Receiving this kind of information from the Spirit takes practice. It is the same for words of knowledge about healing—both inner healing and physical healing. Having such a word greatly increases the receiver's faith for a miracle or life change.

As you grow in discernment, it will affect every aspect of your ministry. You will know better how to hear the Lord on where to go and on when and where to meet certain people.

Jesus, as always, is our example. His seemingly untimely decision to wait two days before going to pray for Lazarus brought forth power ministry to a whole town (see John 11). Another time, Jesus released power ministry by putting the unbelievers out of the house before he prayed to raise a little girl from the dead (Mark 5:40).

Of course, as in any training, there is trial and error. My friend, Heidi Baker, whose ministry in Mozambique has seen more than 30 dead people raised and thousands of others healed of deafness, blindness, and more, tells how she prayed for the first 99 people with no results. The 100th was healed instantly. Another friend, Stacey Campbell, received numerous prophetic words that God was going to use her in a major healing ministry. For more than 10 years, little happened when she prayed. But she kept praying. And now she is consistently walking in signs, miracles, and wonders—and she's glad she didn't give up!

Practical Growth

In addition to reading the Bible as a training manual for operating in power ministry, you should also read accounts of the lives of those who have operated in it. Learn and dream with God about your desires for the miraculous, and discover how others have moved into it successfully.

You might also sit under the teaching of ministries that model what you desire to do. Learn from their style, format, and results. This doesn't necessarily mean that you have to change churches or move to a different city. In this media age, you may be able to simply sign up to receive their weekly teaching or watch their services on video streaming or television.

Another wise choice would be to attend some of the new "power ministry" schools. These programs cost less and are shorter than conventional Bible schools, and they focus more on teaching and training in the use of the power gifts. They prepare you in a shorter time to put your dream to work on the mission field, in your downtown area, or in your neighborhood, school, or workplace.

Attend every good conference that you can on the supernatural and those that offer impartation of the power gifts. Buy the CDs or DVDs if you are not able to go. You would pay for and attend a university course on a subject that you needed to learn, and this mode of learning is cheaper and easier to use.

Take every opportunity to minister, and ask regularly for feedback and correction. Try a home group before you jump into the pulpit. Do you love healing and miracles? My friend Bill Johnson says we should consider those with crutches, casts, and wheelchairs as "fair game." Hardly anyone will turn you down if you sincerely and politely ask if you can pray for them.

Go to nursing homes, homeless shelters, and jails to put your gifts to work. Hone the skills that make your initial approach successful so that you don't turn people off before they can see Jesus in you.

Grow up in your level of faith by simply exercising your gifts and obedience. If possible, join a mentor program or request mentoring from those who currently minister in your areas of interest so that you can be more personally trained.

Make use of the power of the testimony. Read as many books as you can about miracles and power ministries, including biographies of the great revivalists. These works will fuel your faith and your passion. You will also find that they will build your confidence that you too can do the greater works that Jesus referred to (see John 14:12).

Always Remember...

In our quest for ministry that delights God and surely delights us, we must never forget the apostle Paul's greatest pursuit: *"That I may know Him, and the power of His resurrection, and the fellow-ship of His sufferings..."* (Phil. 3:10).

Our intimacy with the Lord is our greatest purpose and delight. From that place, everything else that is meaningful or lasting flows. You will move in power ministry when you are intimate with God. That's His *modus operandi*. As we partner with Him, we will see individuals, cities, and even nations transformed for His soon return. Come, Lord Jesus!

ENDNOTES

1. Dr. Bill Hamon, *The Day of the Saints* (Shippensburg, PA: Destiny Image Publishers, 2005).

2. John Wesley, quoted in Dutch Sheets, *Intercessory Prayer* (Ventura, CA: Gospel Light, 1996), 23.

About Che Ahn

Dr. Che Ahn and his wife, Sue, are the Senior Pastors of Harvest Rock Church in Pasadena, California. Che and Sue have four adult children, two of them married, Gabriel, Grace and Steve Baik, Joy and Kuoching Ngu, and Mary.

Che is also founder and president of Harvest International Ministry, a worldwide apostolic network of over 5000 churches in over 35 nations with the common vision of "Changing Lives, Transforming Cities, and Discipling Nations."

Che received his MDiv and DMin from Fuller Theological Seminary and has played a key role in many strategic local, national, and international out-reaches, including being the President of TheCall from 2000-2004.

Che is author of numerous books including *Into the Fire, How to Pray for Healing, Spirit-Led Evangelism,* and *Close Encounters of the Divine Kind.* He travels extensively throughout the world, bringing apostolic insight with a Holy Spirit impartation of revival, healing, and evangelism.

BOOKS BY CHE AHN

Into the Fire
The Authority of the Believer and Healing
The Call Revolution
Hosting the Holy Spirit
How to Pray for Healing
Spirit-Led Evangelism
Say Goodbye to Powerless Christianity
When Heaven Comes Down
Journey to the Father's Heart
The Grace of Giving
God Wants to Bless You
Remarkable Miracles, Unusual Signs
The Mystery of Loving Jesus Christ

NOTES

Made in the USA
Monee, IL
13 August 2022